Let's Sit Down, Figure This Out

Let's Sit Down, Figure This Out

Prose Poems

Grant Kittrell

groundhog
POETRY PRESS

2017

Library of Congress Control Number: 2017953310

ISBN: 978-0-9976766-7-9

Printed in the United States

Published by

Groundhog Poetry Press LLC

6915 Ardmore Drive

Roanoke, Virginia 24019-4403

www.groundhogpoetrypress.com

The groundhog logo is the registered trademark ™
of Groundhog Poetry Press LLC

Contents

In The Dirt

I took a drive out to The Gallimaufry Goat Farm and was struck by the vast assortment of goat life in one place. Goats who'd go shock-still when startled, like a bolt through the head, fall stiff as taxidermy to the ground. Others, preferring a higher form of life, would scale the argon trees, hoof the branches like acrobats, munch away at leaves while visitors meandered below. Other goats, the most peculiar kind of all, marched around bleating in the voices of men. Some goats were just normal goats. The whole combination of them in one place left me starry-eyed and awestruck. This crazy little farm with its hodgepodge of goats represented, in my mind, every facet and variety of human existence, a universal model for the living world—I was all wrapped up in metaphor! And I was just about to figure the meaning of it all when a well-endowed buck, trunks for horns, came by and knocked me in the dirt. One goat who'd been grazing nearby witnessed the scene and fainted on the spot. Another bounded off a high branch, glided down and hovered in the air just overhead. He looked down at me, stoic-like it seemed, with his panoramic pupils, and screamed.

Aiming

My left eye does different things than my right. By that I mean, while pointing my finger in one direction—say, at the dimple that cradles your smiling—I can also be pointing at your ear or something, if I switch eyes. We were skeet shooting when I learned this, in the iris of Blakely, GA, where the distance between things—say, the distance between two fields, or, say, your house and mine—doesn't mean as much. The conversions aren't the same. If you're shooting at a clay disk, for example, switching eyes is the difference between hitting a clay disk and hitting blue air. No one gets hurt. If you're shooting at a varmint, it's the difference between hitting the varmint and hitting a blade of grass. But if you're shooting at the sea, you come to find out when you make it back to the coast, it's still only the difference between hitting the sea and hitting the sea. The same goes for the sky, pardoning a stray and unfortunate cloud. I could be pointing at you or I could be pointing at you. I like the idea of pointing at two things at once. I like to cross my eyes from time to time, too. And then, other times, I like to close them.

Everyone's Pregnant

On this full-bellied day in Hartford, Connecticut I am walking around smoking a cigarette thinking of all the ways I could make a thing. My cat is pregnant. His name is Mother and he's a real mother fucker of a brute. He's done all the right things, apparently. He's been following all the lovely girls around town wrapping them up in his own way and he's as wide as a snowstorm. My igloo is getting warm in here too. It will not be long before it is not an igloo and thus my little one will not be a little one. Everyone's all walking around here blown up. I am thinking about tying strings to them all just in case. It's a cold morning in November and my shoes aren't doing the job. A girl my age passes pregnant and I place my hand on her belly. We are in an alley sharing a cigarette and she reaches out and touches mine. We are spinning smoke and talking about the next move and the effects on third trimester. We are waiting for the blow. Last time the explosions were slow and from the inside, then the city went up in its first cry. We are waiting for the first cry. Me and this girl.

Papa's Crispies

are still popping. But at the kitchen counter he's getting all soggy and she's getting soggy and they know it and sometimes they do not pop at each other like they used to. After the open heart he's lying there deflated in the hospital bed, and she comes in and she's looking at him hard, like the body goes when a balloon pops unexpectedly, but slower to compose. And as much as they pop at each other back home, as noisy and as mean as he can be, when he's lying in that bed you can see she's afraid the popping will stop. Because she knows that a crispy takes more than a crispy to pop. I put an ear to my bowl, sitting there by Papa at the kitchen counter and listen to my crispies and they make the same sound as Papa's, though not quite as loud because Papa uses the big bowl. I wonder what happens inside him when he finishes all those crispies, if the popping inside him has something to do with his keeping going. When she does not cook him his eggs and his bacon and his toast and jelly, she always gives him the crispies, and I wonder now if she knows something I don't about the nature of popping. I take a mouthful, hold the crispies on my tongue and tilt my head back like I'm screaming. I'm not screaming, I'm just trying to understand.

What They Did

A man had a little bit of god in him, didn't know what to do
with it. Let it sit there and be. That's what the doctor said.
No sense trying to fix something that doesn't need fixing. Let
it be. That's what he did.

A little bit of god had some man on him, didn't know what to
do with it. No cure for this, the doctor said, but a verbal lub-
ricant will relieve the pain every time. Say what you will.
That's what he did.

A doctor had a little bit of god in him, some man on him too,
threw a party to celebrate the union. We gather here today to
celebrate this blessed union. That's what the doctor said.
Let's glorify it into the night. That's what they did.

There's A Man Here
With A Hemingway Inside

His chair is shrinking beneath him on the coffee shop patio. I
should grow a mustache, a full-blown beard. This brisk No-
vember means nothing and everything to his smoky sail of
hair. He runs his fingers through it like a god. His wife hasn't
said a word since they arrived. He is one with the beagle at
the next table over, casts a pensive gaze to stroke its head. I
need to reassess the legitimacy of my sunglasses. He fingers
the lip of his favorite shotgun, the eye of his father's fishing
rod, bearing the sway of experienced hands. She is watching
the pedestrians. She does not look at him. He is kissing the
muzzle of his French roast. I have known a woman who
loves the thick and curl of my chest hair—button down,
button down. The lioness of his dreams comes bounding up
Center Street. He drops all but his gun to chase her. A wom-
an stands naked at the bathroom sink, light and dizzy, con-
templating the man who holds her in the mirror. I am float-
ing among the leaves of his contrails, kicking his empty can
of fishing worms down the sidewalk home. She is waiting
there. The wind is picking up.

Off The Dock

Things are not always dead. Dad's elbow, for instance, I
thought I saw it folding in the shallows among the orange
tree scraps. Mom dumps them off the end to float the creek.
There's a tide here. Some things get stuck in the mud, or hold
like rusted lures to oyster beds. I used to swear I caught
something worth hollering about, fishing with Dad along the
edge, hooked on a shell, pulling until the line broke. But there
are no ropes tied to these trimmings, no telling where they'll
land. Like his bird-limbs at night, tossing to the side in shal-
low sleep, she'd have to watch them. Work never left, hung
thick as gulls off the end. They think Mom's throwing out
food scraps. She does sometimes—old meat, molded bread,
mashed potatoes. These birds just want to eat, know what it
means to survive for each other. But seagulls, they get disap-
pointed too. There's no life in these limbs, not the kind they're
looking for. But then I thought I heard Dad yelling from
down the creek, the wheelbarrow squeaking to the end again.
I saw an orange tree sinking beneath the tide, wrapped like a
barnacle in the dock line.

If You Take One Buttercup

What do I think buttercup is? Buttercup is candy first, then a
flower that you put under your nose to figure something
out. I use to know how to feed a horse. I have an idea now
though the theory may be outdated. I haven't tested it.

For snow, there is one way to solve the problem of Floridian:
grocery bags over those sandals. I have a knife dad gave me
on a road trip to Miami, in case Crazy Eyes came through
the window, that kind of thing happens in Miami. I have
never stabbed a living soul in my life.

"God," a stranger said, "bless you!" and I turned around and
thanked her. Someone said, "bless your heart," and, "my
ass," I added, "too." It's cold in here! Someone called me a
"hopeless Floridian" but I don't know what that has to do
with me.

Those horses back at Papa's never had a time. Of course I'm
not sure what that has to do with me either. But if you feed
a horse an oyster he'll grow ten inches. His tail, his tail!
Don't jump on the back of your conclusions. Let's sit down,
figure this out. I got a buttercup in the back seat that needs
your nose to see itself.

Out Of The Wood

I'm driving through no man's land and this Bull moose
(where did this Bull moose come from? is this Canada? (how
the hell did I get in Canada? during the war? (what war did-
n't I fight in? was I a coward? (who raised me to be a coward,
my dad? (where is my dad, back in the Lone Star? (what's he
doing in the Lone Star, did he hide after the war? (what war
didn't he fight in, the French Revolution? was he French?
(how was he French? was he born in a cereal bowl? (have I
eaten today? (what day is today, the Fourth? (how did it get
July so quickly, was I sleeping? (where did I fall asleep, in
Canada? in the Lone Star? (why was I so sleepy? all the side-
stepping? the medicine? (what kind of medicine? for the
pain? (where did it all this pain come from?)

At Home With You

On the coffee table, piled and scattered, some sort of red berry, pine needles, a little buttercup, I think it's called. Along the bookshelf, weed flowers, weed flowers. The window sill, dandelions, leaves of maple.

On further note, to say something about myself. Who I am, would like to be, for you. When you come into my home, to say, without naming, who I am: I am a man with flowers. Things of nature, pinecones, see? And other things.

I will bring you inside and set you down by the little yellow flower. Now.

Be that for me. Be this for me.

Something Happened

After that, the town sat still, watched a crow pass in its horizontal way. Then everyone fell to sleep. That's what happens when the future meets gravity at the top of the fill. Things start tipping. I once humped over, got the best grasp I could of the earth to hold it still. Little grass reins. But people kept screaming at me and a dog choked on his own shit. Nothing can ever really happen here. When the crow falls and the cattle squat on their hindquarters at daybreak, they are protesting the next scene. I don't want to talk about the future any more. It isn't any fun. I want to talk about the way your hair smells when you haven't washed it in a few days. That's the only way that anything can ever happen. We'll bury ourselves one by one into each other. Sit into it, make our graves of things already dead, and feel okay about it.

Smart Toe

Smart toe waves at me from the coffee table. I like when smart toe waves at me. I can read her better than any other. Smart toes are easy. They just wiggle around and that is sufficient for thought. I can say to smart toe confidently, I know what you are thinking! and smart toe will wave back as if to say, you rascal, you caught me! Sometimes smart toe wiggles unprovoked. And then I get suspicious. What are you thinking about smart toe? Sometimes I wonder if something besides smart toe possesses smart toe. Just when I begin to think it's just me and her, smart toe moves unexpectedly and I'm sitting on the couch with smart toe out in front of me and I'm like, Smart toe! What's gotten into you? And she wiggles around a little more and I am usually satisfied with that. In that way I think it's the strongest of bonds we have, smart toe and I. One of these days, when I'm ready, I'll buy her a smart toe ring to seal the deal. I can only hope that when that time comes, she will wave back to me.

A Place To Swim

You coming in? she asked him. I'm waiting for the atom
bomb, he said. But blood flows in one direction. I flow in two.
Who are you waiting for? I'm waiting for the Buddha. Who
are you waiting for? I'm waiting for you, babe. To divide in
half?—

—Jesus Christ, the good cell, look! Sinking in again. She was
sitting on the creek rock. Sinking in again. I'll pray to the
Buddha. I'll pray to the water flea. What are you waiting for?
I don't know. What are you waiting for? A right time.

You coming in? she asked him. I'm waiting right here. You
going to run? No. You going to take off? No, right here. I'm
stone cold, she said. No, you're good, you're a good cell.

I'm cold, she said.

The Orange Peel

There's a fruit giveaway on the corner and your friend she takes a couple and pretends to juggle. You're only juggling if you have at least three oranges. That's okay, she says, at least I'm good at peeling. The giveawayer says if you can peel an orange in one go you'll be a good mother and that sounds about right. My friend tears her orange peel all to pieces but she gets the job done. Well, is there any credit for speed? she asks the giveawayer. Speed is relative, he answers, to the number of oranges you can peel at one time. My friend peels eighteen oranges at once and stuffs her face like an Olympian. We all gather around her broken piñata and dance among the trimmings. This is the way the world can only work. This is the orange peel, the ornament for the ages.

Return To Bryson City, NC

The moment I broke from Mom at Deep Creek, I don't remember. Whirling whitewater at three-years-old on a rubber inner tube—her hands held the rope that held me close. Did her grip slip from the weight I was becoming over those knee-high falls? Or did she trust the creek in a way I could only trust her back then? What freedom did she have to give me, so young in letting go? At some point I found myself without a tube, bobbing the cold will of Swain County. But even this I just barely remember. Sometimes the rescue makes irrelevant the disaster—the hands of strangers, lifting me by the shoulders of my life jacket like a couple of Cherokee angels. "I never thought I'd see you again," I cried to Mom, alive in her hands—I remember this as clear as the water rushing by me then.

Gophers And Astronauts

"Gopher the goal," is what I heard and what I sang while an astronaut skipped down the aisle of the church. Us kids danced along as best as we could from the pews.

Vacation Bible School, every summer. After a few years, I thought I was getting the hang of it. Until they threw in this unlikely pair. Not that it bothered me then in the least bit. Give me something to sing, I'd have sung it till the moon burned out. Hell, I'm still singing the tune to this day, "Go, go, gopher the goal…"

But I've been to the moon and back since then—I've had my goals and met them, had some and lost them. And while I can say I've never had a gopher for a goal, I now understand the poignant contrast between a hole-dwelling rodent and a space-boogie astronaut, and I think I'm finally getting the hang of it all.

My Squirrels

Have crept through the hollows and peeked into the under-muck. Let me just say that none of my squirrels ever happen twice. That should tell you something about the nature of things. My squirrels are tiny little Buddhas. And if you walk up to one and sit respectfully still, they may tell you a little something something. I'm not gonna tell you shit worth the wait. Do not come sit in front of me respectfully still under the hickory. I may look like the wise wizard of Jacksonville, Florida, I know, but I'm not just sitting there day-dreaming about squirrels! We do not even talk in public! I am not psychotic. Though what's the use in telling you this, just ask my squirrels. They will tell you I am not psychotic. They may or may not talk to you in public but the talk is worth the wait when it comes to squirrels. Go sit beneath that hickory there and just start talking. You may look psychotic but believe me, you're not. A nut of some kind comes in handy. Preferably a peanut, preferably boiled. Do not bring a pecan. My squirrels won't tell you a damn thing with a pecan. If they do start talking, sit respectfully still and listen up. Believe it when they tell you to believe nothing I have told you. My squirrels are not liars. They are as close as you'll get to the truth.

My Squirrels

are desperate. They take what they can get these days. A
sunflower seed will do it, or a corn nibble. Just be careful
what you say. They've lost their line. They've taken to the
street under the guise of mice. You say a mouse and a squir-
rel are virtually the same thing but you may have just lost
your mind. Yesterday, I saw a squirrel march straight
through a construction site, right between two hard hats. Did
I mention my squirrels are courageous as hell? The two men
got a kick. I got a kick. One said, he's got some nuts walking
in here! and I smiled so wide I had to look away. I started
thinking about the disproportionate size of squirrel genita-
lia—they really are huge—and marveled at this transaction
between such distant spirits. Amidst it all, my squirrel
turned to me and said, *go do what you have to,* and I listened.

My Squirrels

are in danger. It's hunting season for the kids. They show
their fathers what they're made of. When I was younger, be-
tween the fields of north Georgia, I shot a Robin out of the
high branch of a pine, but that wasn't enough. There's a lot of
life to get through. Grandma, she went out in a bed five
states south of here. It was easy, from what I've heard. I was
not aiming a Daisy at her head. My older cousin shot at a tree
until it bounced straight back through the sight of her barrel.
She wasn't blinded, thank goodness, and I am not a killer,
thank goodness, thank goodness. I am shooting trees on far
off planets, where the likelihood of hitting a squirrel is espe-
cially low, and the possibility of ricochet is almost non-
existent. Come shoot with me, kid, when you've finished
talking. I'm not as crazy as I look. Come shoot and see what
happens.

My Squirrels

have detected our sorrow. Listen—I once told a man I was
sorry, and he leaned over the counter, stuck his nut-like fin-
ger in my face and said, never say you're sorry. Say, *forgive
me*. Say, *I apologize for the inconvenience*, but never say, I'm
sorry. I'm sorry. I'm so sorry, squirrels, to inconvenience you
but I *am* sorry. That man was on vacation, talking himself out
of a divorce. I remember him Jewish, come to think of it. And
I say, I feel it in my bones, too, old man, and he pats me on
the back and we step outside and have a beer together. But
this means very little to my squirrels. I tell them I am happy. I
say that I'm sad. I say, I've climbed the tallest redwood! I say
I love you, love you all for calling me down. Please forgive
me.

My Squirrels

line like teeth in the hickory and breath prophesy. This isn't a performance. They're not here to entertain you. I once told a classroom of students that it was *not* the center of the universe. I fingered the ledge of my throat, a missing wisdom tooth, and insisted: *this* was the center, until they took it away! Who knows where it is now, but it certainly isn't in *this* classroom—five stars to the person who finds it. I sometimes like to think of myself as a squirrel. I once told this to a room full of respected peers, but think I made it up on the spot for a laugh. It worked, and I've believed it ever since. Aren't we all just here to entertain each other? Unfortunately, my squirrels are not impressed. I say: Squirrels, sometimes I like to think I am just like you, and they turn their heads and bark. Despite this, sometimes I like to think I have swallowed my wisdom, that it has lodged itself permanently on a rib or something, that it grows there like a nut. One day my squirrels will take notice. For now they just keep barking.

My Squirrels

are still waiting. Have you talked with them? Have you initi-
ated the conversation? If not, they may be getting anxious,
and they are not by nature skittish creatures. This time last
year I told them you were in search of the truth. I told them
to keep eyes for the helpless one. They came down from their
arches two months later confused and out of focus. We can-
not differentiate, they told me. The sadness below is suffocat-
ing. You will know, *you will know*, I insisted, and then felt
ashamed for speaking in such a way to my squirrels. For they
hold the last and only truth. I myself have lost touch these
days. Let's all gather 'round—you and me and squirrel and
you and me and squirrel—and sing *haba laba laba* for the hick-
ory that holds our organs, as one, in working place, until the
fox has passed. *Haba laba laba, haba laba laba.*

I Am Having Fun

We're walking the dog and this kid's bumming a ride on his
mama's bike and he states it like a pale truth: *I am having fun.*
We look at each other, then kick the linguistics can all the
way home. Let's consider the rhetorical situation: a half-
renovated neighborhood, a mama who should've put her kid
on a bike long ago, and a windy day to blow him right back
off—*hell yeah*. Don't say what you don't mean it's not funny. *I
am having fun.* Don't say it if you don't mean it. The alpha
robin in the backyard is the most beautiful thing I have ever
seen. He looks just like a lion. But he's not having fun. My
dog's about to lasso a rope around my neck and walk me
down Highland Avenue. He is not having fun. I am watching
the wind fling open the screen door out of obligation to the
forecast. It's not having fun. I don't know what to do any-
more. I'm resorting to a hickory nut and a homemade sling-
shot—for the bird, for the dog, for the wind, but especially for
that goddamn kid.

Kettle Number 40

After brewing 39 kettles of tea, kettle number 40 tipped over and scalded my hand to the bone—well, not really to the bone, but it hurt bad enough—hurt so bad I shouted louder than I did five years ago when I won the lottery back in Florida and went out and bought 30,000 dollars worth of tea. I only had a little left tonight, but I had enough to make a few more kettles and that's what I was going to do. But at kettle number 40, the kettle tipped over and scalded my hand to the bone—well, not really to the bone, but it hurt pretty bad. After I finished shouting, I looked down at the teakettle and asked why it had done such a wicked thing and it said that I'd had enough. It said that obsession drives people to do horrible things and that I should learn to contain myself. That's a reasonable thing to say, I said, then asked why it didn't take its own advice and it just sat there on the counter and didn't answer me.

A Proper Speed

The last thing the bear expected was to be stopped by a policeman as he was moseying across the road from one forest to the other. But as it happened, he was stopped by a policeman, and having never encountered one before, found himself in a state utter bewilderment. "Bear, do you know how fast you were going?" "Uh, well, no sir—but I was walking at the same speed I always do." "Well," said the officer, "your normal speed isn't fast enough in these parts. The speed limit's fifty-five on this road, and I'd say you were dawdling at about three." "But I can't run fifty-five mph," said the bear. "These stubby legs can only carry me so fast. And where would I be going at that kind of speed anyway?" "Nowhere in particular," said the officer, "but you got to be moving there faster than you just were. I'm going to have to give you a ticket." The officer handed the bear a ticket, which of course the bear had no idea what do with. "Put it in your pocket," said the officer, "and let me show you how to move at a proper speed. Here, let me tie this rope to your front paws and pull you behind my car. You'll get the hang of it in no time." The officer pulled a rope out of his trunk, tied it to the front paws of the befuddled bear, then climbed back in the driver's seat and began to accelerate. Before he knew it, the bear was moving at the proper speed, was tossed and beaten by the pavement underneath him. "Pick them feet up, bear!" the officer hollered out the window, "Move them legs!" Pick it up! Pick it up!" But the bear couldn't do a thing. He'd lost all control of himself, wanted nothing more than to slow down and walk back untied into the tranquil forest. So when the police car finally slowed at a crossing, the bear did the only thing he could think to do: he reached out with his mangled, road-burned back paws and wrapped them around a nearby root. And when the car started rolling again, making its way toward the city, the bear never let go.

Nana

We talked about bodies and souls. I asked the simple question: where do they meet? Well, she replied, we have two souls, they're under our feet, and I, laughing, long with the thought kept driving.

The Trees Are All Falling

We congregate in the open spaces to call the next move. Some baby points to a far live oak and everyone cocks their heads to see. "It's all over!" Dofrie says, and we howl with delight. I was resistant to the movement myself, but yesterday I must have been in the right place, at the right time, because I just couldn't help the untethered echo of the heart when it came a -tumbling. This must be what it's like to meet God. This autonomous, perfect falling. I can't even sleep at night. I want to be standing all the time. I want to know what happens when I'm not looking.

They Made It

Someone took to the sky and we all sat there like it was easy. Leaving it behind's not always easy, but there's something in the creak and pull of a lawn chair that makes the rest seem to move just for our pleasure. A gull swooped by. Someone was fitting more easily into the blue, and this made drinking easier, with our heads crooked up. If you have an extra dollar or so, purchase an old fashioned lawn chair, the kind that doesn't rust—leaning back in anything less is the opposite of taking to the sky. Someone disappeared up there. We all grew dense from the weight of the space between us. Soon enough, our lawn chairs would sink into the beach sand, leaving only our heads in sight. If we squinted our sunburnt eyes long enough, we thought we could see the grain of someone swept up in the atmospheric tides. We let our heads fall back to the sands, told the fiddling crabs they'd made it.

On The Front Line

When Nelson invited me to join him in a Civil War battle reenactment, I couldn't turn him down. I put on the uniform, learned to flip a gun around, and followed the troops into the battlefield. As we were taking our positions on the front line, he turned to me and asked if I was ready. I said I was, and winked an eye at him. "Why did you wink?" he demanded, "This isn't any time for joking around!" "What do you mean?" I asked, "I thought all this was just for show!" "It is," he said, "but that doesn't make it a joke. Is your gun loaded?" "Loaded?" I asked, "Why on earth would it be loaded?" A car alarm was going off somewhere in the parking lot. "Here," Nelson said, dropping three lead slugs in my hand. "Don't waste them, that's all you got." "Wait, I'm not going to kill anybody!" I shouted, then went quiet. The other soldiers were glaring at me now. "Yes," he ordered, "you are." So I loaded my gun and prepared for the inevitable. The drums were beating a battle tune into the morning air as the onlookers began to cheer. I clenched my musket tight. I felt my instincts firing—I'd been waiting for this moment all my life. It was 1863 and the sun was shining. A baby cried and a plane flew overhead as the attack came from up the hill.

Gnats

"That's what you do when you get old," Nana says, "you go out on the porch and watch the cars drive by. Don't know what we'd do if we hadn't that barn to attend to—and the dust from the fields, it covers everything! We'd wait for lunch, wait for dinner, wait—" Papa butts in, "Wait for the news to come on!" "The gnats are too bad outside anyway," Nana continues, "and there's mosquitoes too! Yesterday we were sitting out on the porch and they just covered my arms, like moles, got all in my eyes! I don't know where they come from, they're—" "From the ground, Ruby, from the ground!"

Banana Pudding

After the funeral there was talk about what we would eat.
My vote was for a turkey sandwich from the fridge, but
Geoffry wanted something to better fit the occasion. He
wanted BBQ and I told him we'd be standing over his soon if
he didn't watch himself. But we went and we both ate and
had a good time. At the register, Geoffry stopped, slipped a
quarter in the bouncy ball machine. It came out looking like
the world, the Earth world, and I almost thought I saw my
home there. He threw it at Monica who was just coming
through the door. Small world, she said, and I think we both
started laughing. It was funny because of the world. We
stayed and slurped pudding while Monica enjoyed her char-
broiled chicken sandwich. We rolled the world across the
table and bounced it off the ceiling. We stuck it in our
mouths and held it there.

Don't Let The Caterpillar Eat Your Marbles

They take the livewire route and suck'em in. This is a place
we come to find peace. I am not in a mood to suffer. Things
get murky in the down-low. It's a cheap thrill to know that
things are perfect just the way they are. I am not the way I
am. Are you the way you is. You is, in singular portions. I can
only take one at a time. Otherwise, I fill up like a catapult
cushion in the summer time. Where were you when the
blowfish lost its blow? On the coast near Bermuda, sinking
your toes in the sand like the chickens we had as a kid and
buried cause they let us. We are a peaceful crowd. We are the
everlasting fundaments of the non-political political grass
root bursting from your bubble bath. It's a dirty place, cause
we let it. A rusty goo creeping round the corners like monster
blood. We like monster blood. It is our especially special
nutrient. Keeps us catching the bus at the right time in the
mornings. We are fated to forget. I forgot to brush my teeth
today. Maybe tomorrow I will floss. It is less a matter of time,
and more a matter of when the time is right. I am a right time,
all the time. Press the button here. Red is for go.

WiFi Espresso

Some WiFi got in a man's espresso. Excuse me, said the man, I didn't order WiFi in my espresso. No sir, the barista said, you ordered it double with cocoa flakes, whipped cream and a shot of mint. That's right I did, said the man. Well, sir, the WiFi comes free without asking. Well, my espresso tastes funny, grumbled the man. I want another without it. I'm sorry but we don't have any double espresso latte with cocoa flakes, whipped cream and a shot of mint without the WiFi, or any other beverage for that matter. What's that smell? asked the man, looking around. That's the WiFi. My eyes are burning! cried the man. That's the WiFi. What's all that buzzing noise in my head? screamed the man. That's the WiFi. Goddamn I feel alive, cried the man, I like this place! We like you too, said the barista. Now please, go sit down and enjoy yourself.

Oil Change + Inspection

I'm sorry I really just can't hear you because *The Price Is Right*
is alarming from the TV above is the car ready I'm itching to
get along I have to get my hair cut for instance you've won a
round trip to your hometown I have to water the ferns on the
front porch closed captioning brought to you in part by the
following: this is what it can be like to have shingles I'm sorry
but I still can't hear you I feel like I'm spinning my wheel
here my wheels is what I mean you know because of the car
does everything look good as far as you can tell I'm not in the
mood for winning things I just can't have.

Would You Rather

Would you rather kill one cow or thirty chickens? Molly Jean asked. I'd rather kill a cow, I said. Suddenly, out of nowhere, a cow appeared. Molly Jean said, alright then, do it. And I said, but Molly Jean, preferring one possible action over the other doesn't logically necessitate the desire or the obligation to act on that preference. Molly Jean said, that is true, but the world is not a logical place. And I said, sure it is, and then she asked me why the cow was standing in my living room and I said I don't know and I said, I guess you're right. She pointed to the cow, raised her eyebrows and said, now kill it! I said, okay, okay, I'll kill the cow—what do I kill it with? Anything but a gun, she said, you have to slash its throat. I said, I will not slash its throat and have blood all over the place! Molly Jean raised her eyebrows again and I took the knife that appeared in my hand and steadied it for the kill. In a swift and forceful motion, I tore a hole in the cow's throat and closed my eyes, scared to see what I had done. When I opened them, the cow was still standing where it had been before. It didn't fall, it didn't move at all. Inspecting the wound, I noticed there was cotton hanging from the cow's severed neck and I thought, this does not make sense at all. I looked over at Molly Jean and she raised her eyebrows and asked, would you rather be a woman for a year or win 10,000 dollars? I said, I'd rather be a woman, and she raised her eyebrows again.

Charlie Darwin's Nephew

In the mornings, my breakfast comes with a flashbulb circus.
When I find that piece of gristle in my mouth, I have to take it
like a man and swallow. I might be good, but, well— What
will you do now what will you do *now*? they ask. I finish my
strawberry yogurt and walk into a new season. What are you
going to do now? they ask, and I do a cartwheel over the
Brooklyn Bridge. I've never even been to Brooklyn. That
must be why they started following me. You see, I make
things happen, all the time. Just yesterday I tornado-kicked
an old lady in the forehead. I wore the beard of Jesus, of
Charlie Darwin's nephew. I sang "Highway to Hell" to a five
-year-old chemo patient. I am making things happen, every-
day. Everywhere I go, people are always waving at me. They
smile to themselves, hold their breaths long and wait for my
next inconceivable success.

Breaking The Law

I was pushing my groceries to the car when a cart boy pointed to a helicopter overhead. "I wonder who they're looking for," he said. "Don't know," I told him, and continued through the parking lot. It'd been circling the city all day and I'd given it little thought. But as I was loading my groceries into the trunk, I too began to wonder who the helicopter was looking for and, for a moment, feared it might be me. I'd done nothing wrong—I was certain of that. I'd never shoplifted, never once been pulled over for speeding. But what if they knew something I didn't? The growing throb of the helicopter's blade broke my train of thought, and I looked up to see it landing in the parking lot just meters away. A uniformed man stepped out and marched over to me. "Sir," he said, "you're under arrest, come with me." "For what?" I demanded, "what did I do?" "Sir, don't even try to deny that you were afraid we were looking for you." "Well, I won't deny it," I said, "but in what way is that against the law?" He reminded me of an old saying that states if you fear the lion, the lion will come. "I think I've heard of it, but that's not a real law," I told him, "You surely can't arrest me for that! Real laws aren't based on old folk sayings but on logical cases of cause and effect." He quickly pointed out that my fear was the cause and the arrest was the effect. I thought about that a bit: there was a cause, and there was an effect. "Well, maybe you're right about that," I said, "but just because I fear something doesn't mean that fear is a sensible one. The reality of the object of my fear is in no way determined or necessitated by the nature of that fear itself." "You feared us and we came, didn't we?" he asked. "Well—" I thought for a moment, "I suppose you're right about that too. But where are we going? Where are you taking me?" "We're taking you to the place where the law originated, where it applies all the time and to everyone. We're flying people like you in every day." I couldn't stand what I was hearing—the mere thought of living in a place like that—I wouldn't let him take me. I dropped my groceries, pulled out my pocketknife and stabbed the man to death.

Dad Used To Fly Airplanes

He's on a flight back home now, what used to be home, but
he is not the pilot. I hear more than one drone in the air this
afternoon, standing low tide at the end of *his* dock, beside *his*
forsaken skiff hung coon-tracked from cables. I am tracing
the sun's imposing shadow from far away to here. If I squint,
the reflections I see do not have to be glints off sloughs of
water. They could be minnows caught in the tide, Christmas
lights, or stars from a foreign blow to the head. I imagine they
have something to do with the fallen marsh grass here, where
the marsh grass meets bare mud. There's a soft ache behind
my eyes where the stars still burn. Maybe that's what Dad's
meds were for, gazing too long. I'll go see him tonight when
he flies in but I won't ask him about that. He won't be here
long, just a few days to pack. Maybe I'll ask him why the
marsh grass is dying. He'll say he's seen it before, that it's all
part of some ecological chain of events stretching down to
microscopic levels. And he'll be right. Then I'll ask why he's
leaving. He'll say he's going to be happy.

Not So Unlike

The day was not unlike this one. She would say something to him not unlike what he was saying to her now, lying beneath the orange tree. His mother had said something not unlike what they would say to each other, and not unlike the way they would say it. But she had said it a long time ago, in a time not unlike this one, to a man not unlike her son. Not unlike her son in more ways than the son cared to concede, than his mother cared to concede, but not unlike nonetheless. It is true that he did things his father never did, and vice versa. But each did these things in not unlike ways. The world is a different place these days, the father said to his son, something not unlike what his own father had told him, and so on. Things used to be easier, the father had said to his son under the tree, not unlike the one his son was sitting under now, telling her something not unlike what his father had told his mother and meant it, or the way his son meant it now under the tree, the way she would mean it too, a long time ago, on a day not so unlike this one.

The New Place

I say it reminds me of the old Kingsley lake house. It smells like it. I look around. It's all quiet. I look out the window, to the backyard. I sit out on the porch for a long time. I fall asleep there, wake up only when the rain catches my foot. When my sister visits for the weekend, she says she can't believe the place. She says it reminds her of the old lake house. She says you guys are like grownups. She likes the hum of the AC units. I bend my face down in it, smell the air blow out. It smells like the old pop up camper. I feel like I am on vacation all the time these days. I like to sit outside and fall asleep there. I like to watch the birds in the morning. They are vacation birds. They like it here too.

Sunset Poem

If you are staring at the place where the ground meets the edge of your foot, some say there is a horizon there, and sometimes even a sunset. We were drinking margaritas and staring at our feet in Jacksonville, FL in the busy sand, considering each angle. Would the days go quicker if we buried our feet in the sand? What did this mean for the others strolling down the beach? They must have sensed the vastness of our wondering there, because they would come by and gaze down at our feet and say things like, "I use to imagine myself sailing off into that sunset," or "My son used to have a sunset like that," or some would come by and never leave. Sometimes I would start walking home and the sky would be burning its tongue on every step, as I licked the salt from the rim of my glass.

Stupid Trees

Our elderly neighbor's yard is filled with trees that don't know how to be trees. "You stupid tree" he hollers at a palm, whose roots stick in the air and fronds are buried underground. "You're growing upside-down, tree, you're going to make me look like a fool!" The old man places his hands at his sides indignantly. He glances over to our yard where, for now, our trees grow as they're supposed to, then looks back around his own.

He notices the old live oak on the far edge of the property. Its trunk and branches have turned purple today. "No, no, no!" he yells, pacing over. "What the hell are you doing, tree? The whole neighborhood's going to think I've turned soft. I'll be back with the axe, tree, you just watch!"

As the old man turns to head for the axe, the willow by the pond catches his gaze. Instead of weeping loosely beneath, its strands lift instead curled and perky to the sky. "Willow!" the old man yells, "Willow!" as he marches over, "What's gotten into you? You're supposed to look sad and forlorn-like. You look as giddy as a lover. Stupid, stupid tree," he grumbles.

My wife and I watch from an open window as we drink our afternoon tea. He grabs what strands he can reach and pulls to the earth. When he lets them go, they spring back into their unfortunate places. He does this until nightfall, each time with the same result.

But he's a persistent old man. He'll be back out by daybreak, pacing from tree to tree as he always does, cursing the stupidity of which he is unable to rid them. Maybe tomorrow a tree will turn to wax, maybe another will fall—it's always something. My wife and I discuss our sympathies for the man as we watch. But he is a busy man. We do not bother him.

Papa

I call home every now and then, to see how things are going.

"Good," he always answers, "as far as I can tell."

A Stage Of Grief

I was ironing my favorite flannel shirt, the black and rose plaid one with the missing button, when its pocket started bleeding. I grabbed a sterile rag, held it tight over the wound but it wouldn't stop. In the kitchen, the microwave was beeping faster every second and I knew my time with the shirt was running thin. I said my final goodbyes and kissed it on the collar as the beeps blended into a long, perpetual ring. It's time to move on, I told myself when my tears had dried. Besides, I can still use it as a work shirt.

And the next morning that's exactly what I did: I wore it when I mowed the lawn, when I trimmed the hedges, when I watered the eggplant. Then I wore it to Shucker's, to the market and the hospital—I never took it off. When Margie died a few weeks later, I wore it to her funeral. As I entered the church, the preacher noticed the spot on my shirt, rushed up to me, eyes wide, and said, "My God, your heart is bleeding!" I looked down, said, "I think you've mistaken me for someone else," and took my seat.

Down Through The Chimney
Came A Philosopher

He started poking at me about a bunch of things I didn't understand, all crazy babble, like my bub, Graham, who was sleeping in the next room over. So I started at it too, made the same noises he did, as best as I could. The philosopher perked up. Apparently I had gotten on a good point. I started up again. He nodded his head in agreement and grinned like a hound dog. We stood there babbling at each other for a few minutes. Our conversation was really going somewhere, I thought, and maybe Graham would appreciate it too, would understand if he was awake. The philosopher sure was giddy. He pranced around the living room making merry circles around the Christmas tree. A long white beard curled out from his chin and his voice got deep. Every time he liked a sound I made he'd bellow, "Ho ho ho!" This got me suspicious. Who'd he think he was, Jesus? So I made noises with more inquisitive inflections. He stopped prancing and twiddled his feet. I called him over, started talking English, asked him who he was and why he'd come down my chimney. He covered his ears and curled up fetal on the carpet. "What's your name?" I demanded. He didn't answer. "What's your name," I ask again. "God," I thought he squeaked. I could hear my son crying from the other room now. God was crying too. I'd never been much of a father.

I Was Established

in 1989. Before that, I'm not really sure what happened. I'd say my first romance was with a set of leatherback chairs, in the room where I first started wriggling. I saw a bed. Inside was a mama. I saw the ignited lens of a hospital wall. Since then, things have been going alright, I guess: I attended day care, met Smokey the Bear and watched a baseball find its way into the black-holed socket of my little peeper. Someone said: Mind your own business, and I did, from then on. I learned what a man was, but never how to be one. I walked on two legs, like everybody else. I had a bright future, and then I had another one. God was there, and then he wasn't, and then she was. Sometimes, I think, if I were to trace the bases in reverse to those leatherback chairs, I could sit down, and figure out where to be. Come on—I could hear her say it—you are ready to be *here* now.

Following The Goose

He lifts his long neck, looks around the yard as if he doesn't
know he's the early bird. I swear he's mocking me. It's like
he's doing the thing where one of two people who are travel-
ing separately to one place arrives just moments before the
other, and the first leans against a wall, crosses legs and looks
at his or her watch as the other walks up and says "Where
have you been? I've been waiting here for a couple hours
now…"

And maybe that goose has been up for a couple hours. Maybe
he's already eaten, already cleaned himself for the day, if
that's what geese do. But it would be nice, honestly, to wake
up one morning, look out the window and find an empty
yard, to feel I've cracked opened the morning for myself, that
I am not always following this goose into the world, who for
all I know cares very little one way or the other.

But I know that he's not the first one up. Maybe he is think-
ing the same things about the grind of traffic in the distance,
that plane flying overhead holding passengers who woke at
midnight to fly halfway around the globe. Maybe this is why
he lifts his head so curiously every morning.   sit at the win-
dow and admire him for a while. He waddles around a bit
from one side of the yard to the other. He honks here and
there. He sticks his beak in the ground, pulls out breakfast.

I Am Thinking Of All The Ways
I Could Marry Myself

I could marry my earlobe and talk to it. I think it would understand. I could marry my foot, buy it all sorts of comfy shoes. It could walk around with a loving man till death do us part. My belly button. I could marry my belly button. What good it'd do I am not sure, but I could do it—I have to say I am not married to the idea of being married to only one part of myself. If my eyebrows called longingly, I would come. So too would I come, with open arms, to my toenails or genitals, if they called. I am not married to the idea of only being married to part of myself. If at once all my parts called longingly with open arms I would spin around in one place until I was dizzy. I have to say I am not only married to the idea of being married to a part of myself if at this moment, with open arms, something else called.

This Poem Falls Apart

Dad says talking with her's like talking to an iceberg. From a boat or standing on the iceberg? I think: from the boat. From Williamsburg, Virginia, 600 miles from the sunshine state, where Mom drifts aimless through the living room, the nearest iceberg off the coast of Greenland. Dad isn't speaking literally, I know, he just means she's cold—*mom as iceberg* is my own manifestation. I think it is at least. The mind loves absolutes much as metaphor, maybe more, maybe absolutely. He just means she's cold. Cold not like a witch's tit or the weather these days, but cold like –hearted, like –shoulder, like sink your soul, bitch cold. That's all he means, though it's hard telling where one iceberg ends and another ends up. Like the boat, which is also my own. Not my boat, but the idea of boat. I do not own my own, and Dad's is back in Florida, dangling from its lift like a loose tooth. Mom chews on icebergs, evening sweet tea catastrophe until she's wired as the telephone line strung between them, up the east coast, tied high to his mast—not a metaphorical anatomical limb, but the real thing—because it's a sailboat, and he has a sun to disappear behind.

Learning To Drown In The Pacific

Too bad your life raft is made of air, and that a probing
swordfish has surfaced at the edge. No one's ever pegged
you for the melodramatic type—someone dies and you say,
"Well, I guess they're never coming back," which is true, but
God, you don't have to say it like that. It's an easy laugh from
the shoreline, bub, but until you've had a swordfish—sweet-
natured as they are—poking at your inflatable bow, in the
cold, callous waters of Washington State, you might as well
be waving from a Disney Cruise in the heart of the Caribbe-
an. Of *course* they are never coming back. But neither—sorry
to burst your bubble—are you. Because the moon's hired the
tide to give you its tour. On the left you will find a gray wave
shaped like your old papa. On the right, notice the great Kill-
er Whale, with eyes shaped like our next grief.

Acknowledgements

Many thanks to the Jackson Center for Creative Writing at Hollins University and to these wonderful folks for their vital support while putting this book together: Elise Burke, Mark Ari, Cathryn Hankla, April Gray Wilder, Thorpe Moeckel, Molly Jean Bennett, Insley Smullen, Brad Efford, Eve Strillacci, and Michael Loruss.

A Blue Ridge Mountain of gratitude to Richard Dillard.

And thanks to the following publications in which these poems originally appeared:

Construction: "Something Happened"

The Common: "In The Dirt," "Papa's Crispies," "At Home With You"

Perversion Magazine: "A Stage Of Grief"

The Normal School: "Everyone's Pregnant," "Off The Dock"

The Common: *EAT Flash*: "Breaking The Law"

Heavy Feather Review: "Vacancies" Summer 2014: "There's A Man With A Hemingway Inside," "Don't Let The Caterpillar Eat Your Marbles," "I Am Thinking Of All The Ways I Could Marry Myself"

Bridge Eight: "The Orange Peel," "A Proper Place"

Perversion Magazine: "My Squirrels"

Poemeleon: "Would You Rather"

Magma Poetry: "What They Did"

Barely South Review: "Kettle Number 40"

This book was designed and set in Palatino Linotype by
RHWD Industries

Cover art by Ashley Sauder-Miller

Photograph of the author by Rebecca Titus

Printed by Salem Printing

groundhog
POETRY PRESS